Machine Learning for Absolute Beginners

Oliver Theobald

Second Edition

ISBN: 9781520951409

This book is dedicated to my high school maths teacher Jason "Jock" McCollock for his enthusiasm for advanced mathematics and Friday afternoon YouTube cats' videos.

Introduction

It's a Friday night at home and you've just ordered a pizza to be delivered to your home from Joe's Pizza. The squeaky-voiced teen over the phone tells you that your pizza delivery will arrive within next 30 minutes.

But after hanging up the phone, you receive a message from your friend asking if she/he can come over tonight. Your friend doesn't have a car. So you will have to drive over to their house and pick them up.

While of course, you want your friend to come over, it's not good timing. First, you don't want to have wait until the pizza arrives before go to collect her - as the pizza will just sit there on the dining table and get cold. You also don't want to go out to pick your friend up after eating your pizza because then you'll miss your favorite TV episode.

You need to make a quick decision. The first question you need to ask yourself is: *Do I have enough time to pick up my friend before the pizza arrives?*

Remember that the pizza is estimated to arrive within 30 minutes, and if you leave now, you should be back within 25-35 minutes. As you know the route to your friend's house, you can safely predict the journey time with a high degree of accuracy.

But just as you're about to walk out the door you realize there's another variable you have yet to consider. You realize that what you need to predict, in addition to the journey time to pick up your friend, is the time at which the pizza will arrive at your house. This is also something not within your control.

Joe's Pizza is a popular pizzeria, and tonight also happens to be a Friday night. There's a range of factors that could affect your pizza delivery, including how many other people are ordering pizza, how many staff Joe's Pizza has on deck, and the navigation ability of the delivery guy.

These three variables all have the potential to delay the delivery time of your pizza. What's more, this is your first time ordering a pizza on a Friday night. So it's even harder to predict what time your pizza will arrive.

There are three possible methods to tackle this problem. The first option is to apply existing knowledge. However, you have no previous experience of ordering a pizza on a Friday night. Unfortunately, there's also no app to calculate the average wait time on a Friday night for a pizza delivery in your area.

The second option is to ask someone else. This option you have already exhausted. The teenager on the other end of the phone working at Joe's Pizza has already told you that your pizza will arrive "within 30 minutes".

The third option is to apply statistical modelling. Given you've picked up this book on machine learning, let's go with the third option.

You think back to your previous experiences of ordering home delivery from Joe's Pizza. You then apply this information to predict the likelihood of the pizza arriving at your house on time. If the expected time of delivery exceeds 30 minutes then you can justify your decision to collect your friend and return home in time for the delivery guy to arrive with your pizza.

Let's assume you have previously ordered pizza on 8 occasions, and the delivery time was late by greater than 10 minutes on four occasions. This means that there is roughly a 50% chance that the pizza delivery will be late again tonight.

Your mental decision-making process is not comfortable with anything less than 70% (that the pizza delivery will arrive on time). You thus remain at home to wait for the pizza and make up an excuse not to see your friend tonight.

Using existing data to base your decision is known as the *empirical method*. The concept of empirical data-backed decision making is integral to machine learning. Machine learning concentrates on predictions based on already known properties extracted from data.

In this example of the pizza delivery, we only considered the attribute of "frequency," the frequency of previous late deliveries. Machine learning models though consider at least two factors.

One factor is the result you wish to predict, known as the *dependent variable*. In this example, the dependent variable is whether the pizza delivery will be significantly late (more than 10 minutes). The second factor is the *independent variable*, which again predicts whether the pizza will be late but on a different independent variable. Day of the week, for example, could be an independent variable.

It could be a case that in the past when the pizza was delivered on a Monday night the delivery time qualified as 'late'. This could be explained by the fact that Joe's Pizza has fewer delivery drivers on call on Monday nights.

Based on your previous experience, and not withstanding the three late deliveries that occurred on a Monday night, pizza deliveries from Joe's Pizza typically arrive within the estimated time period. This being the case, you could establish a model to simulate the probability that the pizza will arrive late based on whether or not it is a 'Monday night'.

A decision tree can be used to map out this particular example.

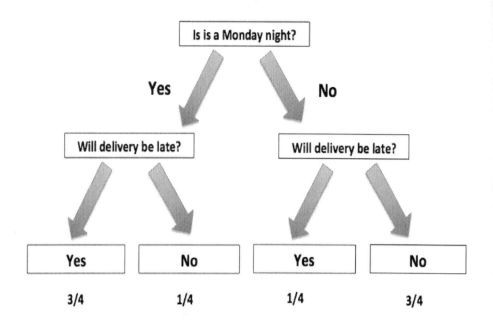

Is is a Monday night?			
Yes		**No**	
Will delivery be late?		Will delivery be late?	
Yes	**No**	**Yes**	**No**
3/4	1/4	1/4	3/4

We now see that under this modelling there is only a 25% chance of the pizza delivery being late.

The process is relatively simple when considering a single independent variable. It does, however, become more complicated to calculate once a second or third independent variable is added to the equation.

Let's now add 'rain' as a third variable which could affect the pizza's delivery time. A rainy night could inherently slow down the delivery time due to safety precautions and extra traffic on the road.

This new variable is added to the decision-making process. The new model now includes two independent variables in addition to one dependent variable.

Dependent variable = Will the pizza be late by more than ten minutes?

Independent variable 1 = Is it a Monday night?

Independent variable 2 = Is it raining?

We now need to predict the number of minutes the pizza will be late based on the level of rain (light = 2 minutes, moderate = 5 minutes, heavy = 15 minutes), and the day of the week.

The predictions produced by this model will give us an idea on how late the pizza will be on any given day of the week. In this case though, a decision tree is of very little use as this model can only predict discrete values (yes/no).

However, with the help of machine learning techniques you can apply *linear regression* to predict the result.

It's now time to sit down at your computer. For the sake of the story let's forget the fact that your friend is waiting for you to reply to their message. Let's also turn our attention to the topic of machine learning.

For decades, machines operated on the basis of responding to user commands. In other words, the computer would perform a task as a result of the user directly entering a command. But as you may know, that has all changed.

The manner in which computers are now able to mimic human thinking to process information is rapidly exceeding human capabilities in everything from chess to picking the winner of a song contest. This leads us into the realm of artificial intelligence and machine learning.

In the modern age of machine learning, computers do not strictly need to receive an 'input command' to perform a task, but rather 'input data'. From the input of data they are able to form their own decisions and take actions virtually as a human would – but of course within the confines set by the machine's operator.

In machine learning, a computer creates a model to analyze the scenario based on existing data (experiences). The model, in this case, is predicting whether the pizza delivery will be late in future cases.

From here the computer treats the data very similar to normal human thinking. But given it is a machine, it can consider many more scenarios and execute far more complicated calculations to solve complex problems.

This is the element that excites data scientists and machine learning engineers the most; the ability to solve complex problems. This is also perhaps the reason you picked up this book, to gain an introduction to machine learning and techniques such as linear regression and decision trees.

In the following sections we will dive in and consider machine learning from an aerial view and discern the relationship between our topic and the larger field of data science. Later in the book I will introduce linear regression and other machine learning techniques without layers of jargon and fancy words as largely found on the Internet.

From Data Science to AI, to Machine Learning

Our study on this topic begins with a high-level overview of where machine learning fits into data science and AI (Artificial Intelligence). Data science is a broad umbrella term that encompasses a number of disciplines and concepts including big data, artificial intelligence, data mining and machine learning.

The discipline of studying large volumes of data, known as 'data science', is a relatively new field and has grown hand-in-hand with the development and wide adoption of computers. Prior to computers, data was calculated and processed manually under the umbrella of 'statistics,' or what we might now refer to as 'classical statistics'.

Baseball batting averages, for example, existed well before the advent of computers. Anyone with a pencil, notepad and basic arithmetic skills could calculate Babe Ruth's batting average over a season with the aid of classical statistics.

The process of calculating a batting average involved the dedication of time to collect and review batting sheets, and the application of addition and division.

The key point to remember about classical statistics is that you don't strictly need a computer to crunch the data and draw conclusions. As you're working with small datasets it is possible even for pre-university students to perform statistics.

Statistics are indeed still taught in schools today, as they have been for centuries. There are also advanced levels of classical statistics, but the datasets remain consistent - in that they are manageable for us as human beings to process. But what if you wanted to calculate numbers at a higher velocity, higher volume, and higher value?

This is where data science and the advent of computers have radically transformed the field of statistics. Modern computing technology now provides the infrastructure to collect, store and draw insight from massive amounts of digitally produced data.

Artificial Intelligence

Artificial Intelligence, or AI as we also like to call it, has also been developing over the same period. It was coined more than sixty years ago when American computer scientist John McCarthy introduced the term during the 2nd Dartmouth Conference in 1956.

AI was originally described as a way for manufactured devices to emulate or even exceed the capabilities of humans to perform mental tasks.

The definition of 'AI' in today's terms remains essentially unchanged, which is based on enabling machines to think and operate like the human brain. AI essentially operates by analyzing behavior to solve problems and make decisions in various situations.

It's interesting to note that the term 'AI' is slightly controversial, in that it tends to confuse or scare those uninitiated to data and computer science.

IBM, for example, have gone to great lengths to disguise AI as 'cognitive thinking' so as not to intimidate the average observer.

As part of a project my start-up worked on with IBM Australia, we featured in a video series exploring the possibilities of 'Cognitive Thinking' in Asia. When we asked IBM why we had to say 'cognitive thinking' instead of 'artificial intelligence' or 'AI', their public relations team said they wanted to stay away from these terms in concern that the average person on the street would associate this with robot-terminators seeking out to kill everyone!

So are the robots really going to take over the world? The portrayal of machines in movies certainly hasn't helped the plight of 'AI'. In addition, and as many have rightly pointed out, man has always found diametrical ways to abuse new technology.

The other problem with 'AI' is that there's a false illusion on parts of the Internet that 'AI' and 'machine learning' can be used interchangeably. Both are popular buzzwords but this is not how a trained data scientist sees these two terms.

Machine Learning

Machine learning algorithms have existed for virtually two decades but only in recent times has computing power and data storage caught up to make machine learning widely available.

Computers for a long time were inept at mimicking human-specific tasks, such as reading, translating, writing, video recognition and identifying everyday objects. However, with advances in computing power, machines have dramatically exceeded human capabilities at identifying patterns found in very large data sets.

Machine learning focuses on developing algorithms that can learn from the data and make subsequent predictions. For example, when you type "machine learning" into Google, it pops up with a list of search results.

But over time, certain results on page one will receive fewer clicks than others. For instance, result three receives fewer clicks than result four. Google's self-learning algorithm will recognize that users are ignoring result three and that entry will thereby begin to drop in its ranking.

Machine learning can be applied independently as in the case of Google search engine rankings, or be applied in data mining on top of other data mining techniques. The following chapters will walk you through specific definitions and characteristics of data mining and machine learning.

Machine Learning

Machine learning, as we've touched upon, is a subfield within both data science and artificial intelligence. Machine learning applies statistical methods to improve performance based on previous experience and detected patterns.

A very important aspect of machine learning is the usage of self-improving algorithms. Just as humans learn from previous experience and trial and error to formulate decisions, so too do machines.

However, not only can machines think and learn like us, but they're also far more effective. Humans are simply not predisposed to be as reliable and proficient at repetitive tasks as computers are in handling large amounts of data. In addition, the size, complexity, and speed at which big data is generated exceed our limited capabilities.

Take the following dataset:

1: [0, 0]

2: [3, 6]

3: [6, 12]

4: [9, 18]

5: [12, ?]

As humans, it's relatively easy for us to see the pattern in this dataset. As the second number in each row is twice as large as the subsequent number to its left inside the brackets, we can comfortably predict that the unknown number inside the brackets on row five will be '24'. In this scenario, we hardly need the aid of a computer to predict the unknown number.

However, what if each row was composed of much larger numbers with decimal points running into double digits? This would make it extremely difficult and near impossible for anyone to process and predict in quick time.

However, this task is not daunting to a machine. Machines can take on the mundane task of attempting numerous possibilities to isolate large segments of data in order to solve the problem at hand, as well as collecting, storing and visualizing the data. Machine learning therefore frees up our time to focus on improving the results or working on other core business.

But how do we program a computer to calculate something we don't even know how to calculate ourselves? This is an important aspect of machine learning. If properly configured, machine learning algorithms are capable of learning and recognizing new patterns on their own.

But machine learning naturally doesn't just start by itself. As with any machine or automated production line, there needs to be a human to program and supervise the automated process. This is where data scientists and machine learning engineers enter.

The role of data professionals is to configure the equipment (including servers, operating systems, and databases) and architecture (how the equipment interacts with each other) as well as programming algorithms using various mathematical operations.

You can think of programming a computer like training a guide dog. Through specialized training, the dog is taught how to respond in various situations. For example, the dog is taught to heel at a red light or to safely lead its master around certain obstacles.

If the dog has been properly trained then over time the trainer is not required and the dog will be able to apply his/her training to various unsupervised situations.

This example draws on a situational scenario, but what if you want to program a computer to take on more complex tasks such as image recognition? How do you teach a computer to recognize physical differences between animals? Again this requires a lot of human input.

Rather than programming the computer to respond to a fixed possibility, such as navigating past an obstacle on the path or responding to a red light, the data scientist will need to approach this method differently.

The machine learning engineer cannot program the computer to recognize animals based on a human description (i.e. four legs, long tail and long neck), as this would induce a high rate of failure. This is because there are numerous animals with similar characteristics, such as wallabies and kangaroos. Solving such complex tasks has long been the limitation of computers and traditional computer programming.

Instead, the data scientist needs to program the computer to identify animals based on socializing examples the same way one would teach a child.

A young child cannot recognize a 'goat' accurately based on a description of its key features. An animal with four legs, white fur and a short neck could of course be confused with various other animals.

So rather than playing a guessing game with a child, it's more effective to showcase what a goat looks like by showing to the child toy goats, images of goats or even real-life goats in a paddock.

Image recognition in machine learning is much the same, except teaching is managed via images and programming language.

For example, we can display various images to the computer, which are labelled as the subject matter, ie. 'goat'. Then the same way a child learns, the machine draws on these samples to identify the specific features and patterns of the subject.

Whether its recognizing animals, human faces or even illicit material, the machine can apply examples to write its own program to provide the capability to recognize and identify subjects. This eliminates the need for humans to explain in detail the characteristics of each subject and dramatically mitigates the chance of failure.

Once both the architecture and algorithms have been successfully configured, machine learning can take place. The computer can then begin to implement algorithms and models to classify, predict and cluster data in order to form future predictions and draw new insights based on patterns.

Data Mining

Data mining is another popular discipline of data science, and that aims to unearth unknown relationships, patterns, and regularities from large datasets.

Given that data mining does not start with an exact hypothesis as an initial starting point, a myriad of data sorting techniques are applied, including text retrieval, clustering, sequence analysis and association analysis.

A big question for people new to data science is: *What is the difference between data mining and machine learning?*

There is a strong correlation between the two. At an abstract level, both are concerned with analyzing data and extracting valuable insights. In many cases, data mining utilizes the same self-learning algorithms as applied to machine learning. Popular self-learning algorithms such as *k*-means clustering, association analysis and regression are used in both data mining and machine learning.

You might be thinking that given they use the same algorithms and both cast predictions based on historical data, is there any real difference between the two? This is a pertinent question and is not always well explained by data professionals themselves.

As established, both data mining and machine learning focus on forming future predictions based on historical data and very often use the same self-learning algorithms to form these predictions. However, whereas machine learning uses self-learning algorithms to improve with experience at a given task, data mining focuses on analyzing data to discover previously unseen patterns or properties.

Data mining is thus exploratory in nature as it searches for unknown knowledge, whereas machine learning concentrates on studying and reproducing specifically known knowledge to form predictions.

It is also for this reason that the two disciplines diverge in their application. In practice, data mining takes large datasets, cleans the data, and spits out analysis based on relationships and patterns found from the data. It just so happens that machine learning algorithms are a handy tool to clean data, but other algorithms are also applied, including text retrieval.

Data mining renders itself best to large datasets, or big data, and is often a one-off project or conducted at set intervals. Data mining can therefore be thought of as similar to scrubbing oil off rocks and wildlife after a major disaster (to remove undesirable elements) and then sitting back until the next large oil spill.

Machine learning on the other hand focuses on incremental and ongoing problem solving, and fits with solving problems of all sizes. When Google compares your first and second search query and makes an inference on what you are searching for, this is not a matter of cleaning up swathes of data, but rather a gradual process of self-learning.

Machine learning also doesn't turn off once the task is done. It is constantly learning and adapting to new inputs of data – big and small - and storing those values to inform and optimize its future actions. It is this ability to learn from experience over time that makes machine learning an important cog in artificial intelligence, and which is another factor that differentiates machine learning from data mining.

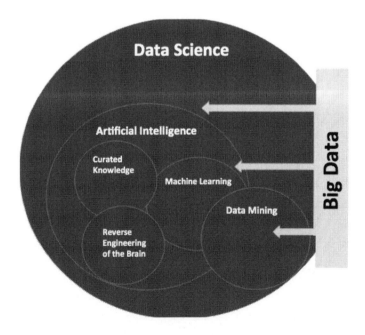

Google's Machine Learning

The world of search engine optimization is changing and machine learning is firmly behind the new face of SEO.

As virtually everyone (outside of Mainland China and North Korea) with access to the Internet can access Google to search the web, Google's new machine learning SEO technology is an easy to digest example.

Prior to the integration of advanced machine learning into search engine algorithms, Google focused their search efforts around strings of letters. Google indexed millions of web pages each day to track their content for strings of letters. This included strings of letters in the webpage title, website menu, body text, meta tags, image descriptions and so forth.

With all these strings of letters and combinations on record, Google could match results based on the string you entered into the search bar. If you typed in "Donald Trump," the search engine would then go away and look for strings in that exact order:

D-O-N-A-L-D T-R-U-M-P

While there are various factors that influence SEO rankings, including backlinks and page speed, string-letter matching has always been a major part of Google's SEO efforts. Webpages containing the exact string of letters entered by the user would thus feature prominently in the search results.

However, if you were to jumble up the letter sequence in any major way, such as T-R-O-N-A-L-D D-U-M-P, the results would differ dramatically.

But Google's new algorithm – backed by machine learning – looks at "Donald Trump" not as a string of letters but as an actual person. A person who has a defined age, a defined job profile, a list of relatives, and so on.

Google can thereby decipher information without just relying on matching strings of letters.

For instance, say you want to search: "Who is Donald Trump's first wife?"

Prior to machine learning, Google would search its online repository for webpages containing those six keywords. However, the accuracy of search results would vary. The search engine, for example, may find an overwhelming number of web pages with keywords mentioning "Donald Trump's wife" "Melania Trump" as the "First Lady" of the U.S.

Google could thereby be tricked into featuring an article regarding Melania Trump on the first page of its search results. The same still happens if you search on Yahoo today.

who was donald trump's first wife

Donald and Ivana Trump's Divorce: The Full Story | Vanity Fair
www.vanityfair.com/magazine/2015/07/donald-ivana-trump... ⌄
Unfortunately for **Donald** and Ivana **Trump**, ... I thought about the ten years since I had **first** met
Donald Trump. ... The Most Fabulous Yachts at Sea BY VANITY FAIR. SEEK.

Why Ivana Trump, Donald Trump's Ex-Wife, Prefers To Date ...
www.huffingtonpost.com/...trump-boyfriends-donald-trump_n... ⌄
Dec 22, 2013 · **Donald Trump's** ex-**wife** Ivana **Trump** ... "Me and **Donald** are very friendly, ... "The
Huffington Post" is a registered trademark of TheHuffingtonPost.com, Inc.

Donald Trump's Ex-Wife Ivana Disavows Old 'Rape' Allegation ...
abcnews.go.com/Politics/donald-trumps-wife-ivana...
Jul 27, 2015 · **Donald Trump's** Ex-**Wife** Ivana Disavows Old 'Rape' Allegation. ... **Donald Trump's**
first wife, ... The Many Lives of **Donald** J. **Trump**." ...

Trump's wife Melania Knauss-Trump a first lady of fashion ...
www.nydailynews.com/life-style/fashion/donald-trump-wife...
The **Donald**'s better half could **trump** every other First Lady. ... **Donald Trump's wife** Melania
Knauss-**Trump** a ... The **Donald**'s better half could **trump** every other ...

Melania Trump - Wikipedia
en.wikipedia.org/wiki/Melania_Trump ⌄
... **wife** of **Donald Trump** and First Lady of the United States. ... Melania **Trump** (born Melanija
Knavs ... **Donald** described their long courtship in 2005: ...

Ivana Trump - Model, Writer, Television Personality ...
www.biography.com/people/ivana-trump-9542158 ⌄
Synopsis. Ivana **Trump** is a former model and **wife** of **Donald Trump** who was born in Gottwaldov
(now Zlín), Czechoslovakia (now the Czech Republic), in 1949.

Source: Yahoo Search

Google though is much smarter thanks to the invisible hand of machine learning. Google is able to decipher words not strictly as strings but as 'things'.

Google knows Donald Trump is a person, and Google knows who his first wife is. It can then processes this information in rapid time to display information regarding Donald Trump's first marriage to Ivana Trump.

Donald Trump's first wife reveals what to expect from his presidency: 'I ...
www.independent.co.uk › News › People ▾
Nov 14, 2016 - While many are busy speculating about what the next four years with Donald Trump as President will look like, Ivana Trump has actually given ...

Donald Trump's family tree: Melania, Ivanka, Tiffany, Eric and more ...
www.amny.com/.../donald-trump-s-family-tree-melania-ivanka-tiffany-eric-and-more... ▾
Jan 20, 2017 - Donald Trump Jr., son. Donald Trump Jr., 39, is Donald Trump's oldest child with Ivana Trump. He serves as an executive vice president of the Trump Organization. Donald Jr. is married to Vanessa Haydon and they have five children.

Ivana Trump - Wikipedia
https://en.wikipedia.org/wiki/Ivana_Trump ▾
Ivana Marie Trump is a Czech-born American businesswoman, author, socialite, and former fashion model. She was the first wife of Donald Trump. ... In October 1990, Ivana Trump's 63-year-old father died suddenly from a heart attack. ... Three years after her divorce from Donald, Ivana married Riccardo Mazzucchelli.

Source: Google

But what's even more exciting is Google's new ability to understand interconnected search queries. For example, say you follow up the next Google search with the question: "Who was his second wife?"

Prior to machine learning, Google would search its online repository for webpages containing those exact keywords. But Google would not be able to connect your first and second search query.

Machine learning though changes the way we search. Now, given that Google already knows our first search query regarding, "Donald Trump", it can thereby decipher the second search query with less specific information provided.

For example, you could even follow up by simply asking: "Who is his wife?" And BANG, Google will come back with results regarding Donald Trump's wife.

Google's new line of learning and thinking is very similar to human behavior, and which is why Google's new technology falls within the field of machine learning and artificial intelligence.

Downloading Datasets

For beginner's starting out in machine learning there are numerous options to source datasets for practicing new algorithms.

While of course it's perfectly fine to source your own dataset from creating a web crawler in Python or using a click-and-drag tool like Import.io to crawl the Internet, the easiest way to get started is with Kaggle.

Kaggle is an online community for data scientists and statisticians to access free datasets, join competitions, and simply hangout and talk about data.

A great thing about Kaggle is that they offer free datasets for download. This saves you the time and effort in sourcing and tidying up your own dataset. Meanwhile you also have access to discuss and problem-solve with other users on the forum about particular datasets.

Below are four free sample datasets you might want to look into downloading from the site to start your own machine learning exercises.

Starbucks Locations Worldwide

Want to figure out which country has the highest density of

Starbucks stores, or which Starbucks store is the most isolated from any other? This dataset is for you.

Scraped from the Starbucks store location webpage, this dataset includes the name and location of every Starbucks store in operation as of February 2017.

European Football Database

Sometimes not a lot happens in 90 minutes but with 25,000+ matches and 10,000+ players over 11 leading European country championships from seasons 2008 to 2016 this is the dataset for football diehards.

This dataset even includes team line up with squad formation represented in X, Y coordinates, betting odds from 10 providers, and detailed match events including goals, possession, goals, cards and corners.

New York Stock Exchange

Interested in fundamental and technical analysis? With up to 30% of traffic on stocks said to be machine generated, how far can we take this number based on lessons learnt from historical data?

This dataset includes prices, fundamentals and securities retrieved from Yahoo Finance, Nasdaq Financials, and EDGAR SEC databases. From this dataset you can look to see what impacts return on investment and what indicates future bankruptcy.

Brazil's House of Deputies Reimbursements

As politicians in Brazil are entitled to receive refunds from money spent on activities to "better serve the people," there's a lot of interesting data and suspicious outliers to be found from this dataset.

Data on these expenses are publically available but there is very little monitoring of expenses in Brazil. So don't be surprised to see one public servant racking up over 800 flights spanning 12 months, and another who recorded R$140,000 (USD $44,500) on post expenses (yes, snail mail).

Tools

Computer programming is an essential skill for budding machine learning engineers and data scientists.

While machine learning is likely to go in the same direction as web development with click and drag software (think WordPress and Wix), computer programming is imperative for anyone wishing to dabble in machine learning today.

To maximise computing performance, C and C++ are go-to languages for machine learning. However, Python remains the preferred programming language for machine learning professionals, as we will soon find out.

Note that if you are already proficient in C and C++ then it would make sense to persist with these two languages if you are not already proficient with Python.

Machine learning demands high computational power and is highly resource intensive. Machine learning algorithms are thus best performed on the GPU (graphical processing unit), rather than CPU. GPU specializes in mathematical operations, including statistics, calculus and matrix algebra, and can be easily accessed these days over the cloud.

C and C++ are the preferred languages to directly edit and

perform mathematical operations on the GPU. However, Python can instead be used and converted into C when used in combination with Google's TensorFlow.

TensorFlow is Google's answer to machine learning and runs on top of Python. As the most popular machine learning framework, TensorFlow supports various machine learning algorithms, neural networks, calculus, and reinforcement learning.

It's possible to run TensorFlow on CPU but be aware that this will be slow to run. For serious machine learning, you should look into investing in a GPU cluster from AWS (Amazon Web Services) or an equivalent cloud provider.

Other relevant programming languages in machine learning include R, MATLAB, Octave, and Julia.

R is a free and open source programming language optimized for mathematical operations, and conducive to building matrixes, and statistical functions, which are directly built into the language libraries of R. Although R is commonly used on the data analytics and data mining side of data science, it does still support machine learning operations.

MATLAB and Octave are direct competitors to R. MATLAB is a commercial and propriety programming language. It is strong in regard to solving algebraic equations and is quick to learn.

However, it is more commonly used in academia than industry. Thus, while you might frequently run into MATLAB in online courses, and especially on Coursera, this is not to stay it's commonly used in the wild.

Octave, on the other hand, is open-source and is essentially a free version of MATLAB developed in response to MATLAB by the open source community.

Julia is a well-designed programming language similar to R, but because it is still relatively new it is not widely used in industry.

As alluded to already, Python remains the overwhelming first choice as a programming language for machine learning.

One disadvantage of C and C++ is that they are difficult programming languages to write, and consume many more lines of code than other languages (such as Python) to achieve the same desired outcome.

Python is easier to learn and operate, and can be used more widely, including in data collection (web scraping) and data piping (Hadoop and Spark). Python via TensorFlow then effectively converts your code to C, and puts in on the GPU to run.

Finally, Python offers access to a number of important machine learning libraries, including NumPy, Scikit-learn, and Pandas.

These machine learning libraries offer you the tools to perform advanced machine learning tasks in Python.

NumPy is free and open source, and is Python's answer to MATLAB, which allows you to manage matrixes and work with large datasets.

Scikit-learn provides access to a range of popular shallow machine learning algorithms, including linear regression, Bayesian inference, and support vector machines.

Pandas enable data to be represented on a virtual spreadsheet that you can manipulate directly from your code. The naming comes from the term 'panel data', which refers to its ability to create a series of panels, similar to sheets in an Excel spreadsheet.

NumPy, Scikit-learn and Pandas can all be used together also. Users can thereby draw on these three libraries to: load their data via NumPy; clean up and perform calculations with Pandas; and run machine learning algorithms through Scikit-learn.

Lastly, to create decisions trees using Python, I recommend you look into downloading GraphViz (http://www.graphviz.org/Download..php).

Machine Learning Techniques

Introduction

There are hundreds of machine learning algorithms/techniques out there to train your data. Popular algorithms include Bayesian inference, association analysis, and neural networks. We will look at a number of these algorithms later in this section. First though we will take a high-level look at algorithm categories.

Machine learning algorithms can be split into different categories, including **supervised** and **unsupervised**. A third category of algorithms is **reinforcement,** but this is an advanced category that students only attempt after grasping supervised and unsupervised algorithms.

Supervised learning

Supervised algorithms refer to learning guided by human observations and feedback from known outcomes. This works by showing data to the machine and the correct value output of the data. The machine then applies an algorithm to decipher patterns that exist in the data, and develops a model that can reproduce the same results with new entry data.

For instance, supposes you want the machine to separate email into spam and non-spam messages. In a supervised learning environment, you already have information that you can feed the machine to describe what type of email should belong to which category. The machine therefore knows that there are two categories available in which to sort the incoming data, and it knows the characteristics of both spam email and non-spam email.

Or to predict who will win a basketball game; you could create a model to analyze games over the last three years. The games could be analyzed by total number of points scored and total number of points scored against in order to predict who will win the next game based on previous performances.

This data could then be plotted on a scatterplot, with 'points for' on the x-axis and 'points against' on the y-axis. Each data point represents an individual game, and the score for each game can be found by looking up the x and y coordinates.

We can then apply linear regression (we will learn this in detail very soon) to predict who will win based on the average of previous performances.

As with the first example, we have instructed the machine which categories to analyze (points for, and points against). The data is therefore already pre-tagged, and we know the final outcome of existing data. Each previous game has a final outcome in the form of the full-time score.

Supervised algorithms operate well by working backwards based on historical data, and are widely used to solve various predictions, including predicting prices for used cars, houses, etc.

For instance, to predict the optimal price of a used car, the supervised algorithm can go back and discern the relationship between car attributes (including year of make, car brand, mileage, etc.) and selling price based on historical data. Given that the supervised algorithm knows the final price, it's relatively simple to work backwards and determine the relationship between cost and the characteristics of the car.

The challenge of supervised algorithms is having sufficient data that is representative of all variations, as well as potential outliers and anomalies. The data used should also be relevant, and if taken from a larger data set should be chosen at random.

Supervised algorithms include Linear Regression, Logistic Regression, Neural Networks, and Support Vector Machine.

Unsupervised learning

In the case of an unsupervised learning environment, there is no such integrated feedback or use of data tags. Instead, the machine learning algorithm must rely exclusively on clustering data and modifying its algorithm to respond to its initial findings - all without the external feedback of humans.

Clustering algorithms are a popular example of unsupervised learning. 'Clustering' groups together data points which are discovered to possess similar features.

For example, if you cluster data points based on the weight and height of 13-year old high school students, you are likely to find that two clusters will emerge from the data. One large cluster will be male and the other large cluster will be female. This is because girls and boys tend to have separate commonalities in regards to physical measurements.

The advantage of applying unsupervised algorithms is that it enables you to discover patterns within the data that you may not otherwise have been aware existed – such as the presence of two different genders.

Clustering can then provide the springboard to conduct further analysis after particular groups have been discovered.

Unsupervised algorithms (without tags) include clustering algorithms and descending dimension algorithms.

Reinforcement learning

Reinforcement learning is the third and most advanced category of machine learning algorithms.

Reinforcement learning is often introduced and explained through analogies to Pac-Man or navigating the unexplored terrain of a video game. As the player that you control progresses through the virtual space of the game, it learns the value of various actions under various conditions. Those learned values then inform and directly influence subsequent behavior within the game. After the virtual space has been fully explored the player can naturally yield faster performance and more optimal results based on its prior experience.

Reinforcement learning is similar, but instead of controlling a virtual player or Pac-Man, you are feeding in algorithms to oversee a machine's progress through unknown data. The major difference in reinforced learning is there is no direct oversight over the machine's learning. Instead, the machine is equipped with reinforcement learning algorithms, and the machine must then fend and learn for itself.

The most talked about example of reinforcement learning is Q-learning. In Q-learning, you start within a set environment of states. In the example of Pac-Man, states could be what challenges, obstacles or pathways stand in proximity to you. In Pac-Man there may be a wall to the left, a ghost to the right, a power pill above - each representing different states. States are represented as S.

The set of possible actions to respond to these states is then referred to as A. In the case of Pac-Man, actions are limited to left, right, up and down movements, and multiple combinations of these four movements.

The third important letter is Q. Q is your starting value, which has a value of 0.

As you explore the given space, two main things will happen:

- Q drops as negative things occur after a given state/action

- Q increases as rewards happen after a given state/action

In Q-learning, the machine will learn to match the action for a given state that generates or maintains the highest level of Q. It will learn initially through the process of random movements (actions) under different conditions (states). The machine will keep track of its results (rewards and penalties) and how they impact its Q level, and store those values to inform and optimize its future actions.

While this sounds simple enough, implementation is a much more difficult task and beyond the scope of an absolute beginner's introduction to machine learning.

However, I will leave you with an example of reinforcement learning and Q-learning following the Pac-Man scenario.

https://inst.eecs.berkeley.edu/~cs188/sp12/projects/rei

nforcement/reinforcement.html

Please note that the following chapters include mathematical equations. Although I have kept these equations as simple as possible, remember that they are shown in this book merely as examples. In practice, programming language can be used to automatically generate and answer mathematical equations. However, I believe it is important to first understand the mathematical background of these algorithms before you move onto programming.

Clustering Algorithms

As mentioned, clustering algorithms are a popular example of unsupervised learning. As an unsupervised learning algorithm, clustering is able to identify tags from training relevant data.

In general, clustering algorithms compute the distance between groupings and divide data points into multiple groups based on their relational distance to one another. Clustering also differs from classification.

Unlike classification, which starts with predefined labels reflected in your database table, clustering creates its own labels after clustering segments of unclassified data.

Analysis by clustering can be used in various scenarios such as pattern recognition, image processing and market research. For example, clustering can be applied to uncover customers that share similar purchasing behavior. By understanding a particular cluster of customer purchasing preferences you can then form decisions on which products you can recommend based on group commonalities. You can do this by offering clusters of customers the same promotions via email or website click ad banners.

k-nearest Neighbors

A simple and easy to understand clustering algorithm is *k*-nearest neighbors (*k*-NN). *k*-NN is used to classify new data points into a category based on their relationship to known data points.

Let's put this into action. Say you have a scatterplot that allows you to compute the distance between any two data points. Additionally, the data within the scatterplot has already been categorized into separate clusters.

Next you drop in a new data point. You can now predict the category of the new data point based on the relationship it has to existing data.

First though you have to set '*k*' to determine how many data points you wish to nominate in order to classify the data. If you set *k* to three, *k*-NN will only analyze the new data point's relationship to the three closest data points (neighbors).

The outcome of selecting the three closest neighbors may return with two Class B data points and one Class A data point. Based on the sample data of our three closest data points determined by *k* (3), the machine's prediction for determining the category of the new data point will be based on the majority of its neighbors, which in this case is 'Class B' with 2/3 of the data points.

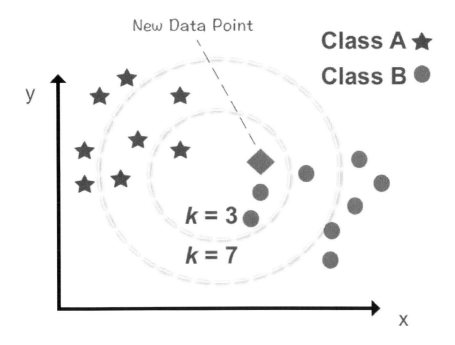

k-NN is similar to a popularity vote or a 'popularity contest', based on what data points are close by. You can think of this as being the new kid at school and choosing a social group to hang out with based on the five classmates sitting nearest to you. Let's say three of these classmates are **data geeks**, one classmate is a **skater**, and one classmate is a **sports jock**. According to k-NN, you would therefore decide to hang out with the data geeks given their numerical advantage.

The choice of your sample data, defined by k, is also crucial in determining your results. Your choice of k will directly affect what new class a point is assigned to. In the scatterplot above, you can see that classification will change depending on whether k is set to '3' or '7'. It is therefore recommended that you try numerous k combinations to find the best fit, and avoid setting k too low or too broad.

A downside of k-NN is that it is computationally intensive to run. This is because it demands storing an entire dataset and calculating the distance between new data points and all existing data points. This algorithm may therefore not be recommended for large datasets.

It can also be challenging to use k-NN with high-dimensional data (3D and 4D) with numerous features. Measuring the multiple distances between data points in a three or four-dimensional space can be taxing on computing resources and complicated to accurately classify.

k-means Clustering

k-means clustering is another unsupervised machine learning algorithm used to identify new clusters based on the attributes of other relevant data.

k-means clustering attempts to split data into k groups. k represents the number of groups you wish to define. For example, if you wish to split your data into three groups then k will be set to three. As part of *k*-means clustering you will need to manually nominate a **centroid** point for each of the three groups.

Below is an example of the *k*-means clustering algorithm in action. The dataset for this example comprises seven bottles of beer (each a different brand) along with two variables: cost price and retail price. In this particular example *k* is set to 2, and thus we are only going to be splitting the data into two clusters.

Bottle	Cost Price ($)	Retail Price ($)
A	1	2
B	3	5
C	5	6
D	5	7
E	2.5	3.5
F	5	8
G	3	4

Step 1: Let's first visualize this data on a scatterplot.

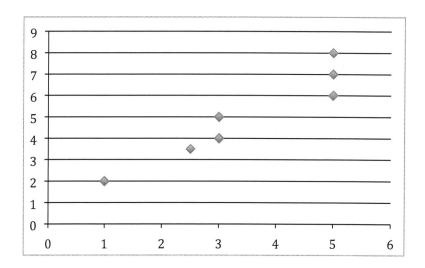

Each data point above represents one beer bottle label, with the horizontal x-axis representing cost price and the vertical y-axis representing retail price.

Step 2: As k is set to 2, the next step is to randomly group the data into two groups. To create two groups we also nominate two data points to act as centroids. You can think of the centroid as a team leader for the group, and to whom the other data points must team up with.

To decide which data points are grouped to which team leader (centroid), the data points will report to the closest centroid based on their own position on the scatterplot.

The centroids can be chosen at random, and in this example we have nominated data points A (2,1) and D (5,7) to act as our centroids. The two centroids are now represented as black circles on the scatterplot below.

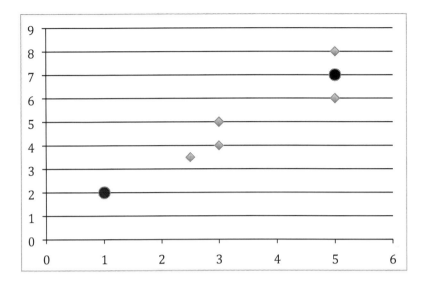

Step 3: The remaining data points are assigned to the closest centroid.

In this example we can determine which centroid is closest by visually reviewing the scatterplot. In real-life though you would calculate the distance between the data points and the centroid using Euclidean distance. But to keep this chapter simple I have left the equation out of the example, and we'll go ahead by assigning our data points visually.

The data points are assigned to the appropriate cluster as outlined in the table below.

Cluster 1		Cluster 2	
Bottle	Mean Value	Bottle	Mean Value
A* (1,2)	(1.0, 2.0)	D* (5,7)	(5.0, 7.0)
		B (3,5)	(4.0, 6.0)
		C (5,6)	(4.33, 6.0)
E (2.5,3.5)	(1.75, 2.75)		
		F (5,8)	(4.5, 6.5)
G (3,4)	(2.16 3.2)		
A,E,G	(2.16 3.2)	D,B,C,F,	(4.5, 6.5)

* Centroid

Cluster 1 comprises A,E,G, and together their mean value is 2.16, 3.2.

Cluster 2 comprises B,C,D,F, and together their mean value is 4.5, 6.5.

The two clusters and their respective centroid (A or D) are now visualized in the scatterplot below.

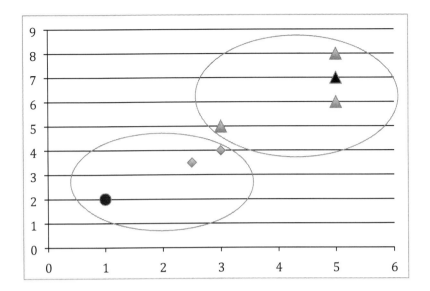

Step 4: We next use the mean value calculated above to create a new and more accurate centroid for each group. The new centroid for Cluster 1 is 2.16, 3.2 (represented as a black diamond on the scatterplot below).

The new centroid for Cluster 2 is 4.5, 6.5 (represented as a black triangle on the scatterplot below).

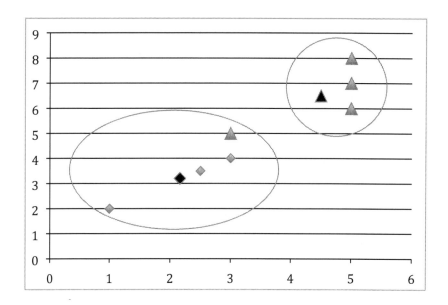

Step 5: We now want to check that each data point still aligns with the updated centroid for its cluster. Immediately though we see that one data point has jumped sides and has joined a different cluster! This particular data point is B (3,5).

This being the case, we now need to go back and update the mean value of each cluster, with B now assigned as a group member of Cluster 1, rather than Cluster 2.

Cluster 1		
	X Value	Y Value
A	1	2
B	3	5

E	2.5	3.5
G	3	4
Mean Average (Centroid)	**2.4**	**3.5**

Cluster 1 now comprises A,B,E,G. It's new centroid is 2.4, 3.5

Cluster 2		
	X Value	Y Value
C	5	6
D	5	7
F	5	8
Mean Average (Centroid)	**5**	**7**

Cluster 2 now comprises C,D,F. It's new centroid is 5.0, 7.0.

Step 6: Let's now plug in our new centroids into the scatterplot. In case you notice we are missing a data point, note that our new centroid for Cluster 2 is sitting directly on top of data point D (5,7).

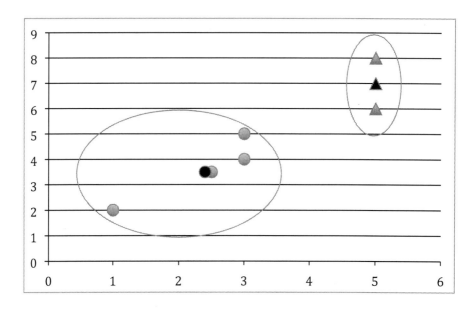

In this iteration each individual data point remains closest to its own cluster centroid, and no data point has switched clusters. This provides our final result. Cluster 1 is A,B,E,G and Cluster 2 is C,D,F.

In this example, it took two iterations to successfully create our clusters. It is important to keep in mind that in some cases *k*-means clustering is <u>unable</u> to identify a final combination of clusters. In such case, you will need to switch tactics and use another algorithm technique to train your data.

Descending Dimension

Algorithms

A descending dimension algorithm is another category of unsupervised machine learning that effectively reduces data from high-dimensional to low-dimensional.

Dimensionality reduction algorithms transform high-dimensional data into a smaller number of dimensions through compression of features, while still preserving as much of the variance in the data as possible.

Dimensionality reduction is thus useful for datasets with a large number of features that can easily be compressed. Also note that dimensionality reduction does not necessarily delete the data, but instead can merge features.

Merging features entails boiling down similar features into one. For example, hotel rooms may have four features: room length, room width, number of rooms and floor level. Given the existence of four features, the hotel room would be expressed on a four-dimensional (4D) scatterplot. However, there is an opportunity to remove redundant information and reduce the number of dimensions to three by combining 'room length' and 'room width' to be expressed as 'room area.' Applying a descending dimension algorithm will thereby enable you to compress the 4D scatterplot into a 3D scatterplot.

Another advantage of this algorithm is visualization and convenience. Understandably, it's much easier to work and communicate information on a 2D plane rather than in 4D.

Another way to perform data reduction is Principle Component Analysis (PCA) and k-means clustering. K-means reduces data variety by boiling down the number of data points into a relatively low number of centroids.

PCA, also sometimes known as general factor analysis, is an unsupervised approach to examine the interrelations among a set of variables. PCA works by creating orthogonal line perpendicular (at right angles) to a linear line. The orthogonal line then takes the role of the new Y-axis. Hint, the new axes will make more sense if you rotate your head 45 degrees to the left.

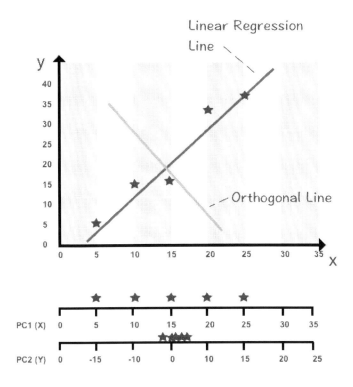

In the scatterplot above we can see that we have two dimensions denoted by X and Y, which are our principle component 1 (PC1) and principle component 2 (PC).

However, based on our new Y axis (created by the orthogonal line) the variance in values of PC2 have been minimized. We can now easily drop PC2 because it contributes the least to overall variance in our new scatterplot. This, in turn, allows us to focus our attention on studying the variance of PC1, which is greater.

PCA is particularly useful in reducing the dimensionality of three and four-dimensional scatterplots, especially as It Is difficult to visually view data points in a high-dimensional space.

Regression

Regression is an important aspect of machine learning. Regression is important as it provides the base for other more advanced machine learning algorithms (including neural networks).

Outside of machine learning, regression is used in a range of disciplines including data mining, finance, business, and investing. In investing and finance, regression is used to value assets and understand the relationship between variables such as exchange rates and commodity prices.

In business, regression can help to predict sales for a company based on a range of variables including weather temperatures, social media mentions, previous sales, GDP growth and inbound tourists.

Specifically, regression is applied to determine the strength of a relationship between one dependent variable (typically represented as Y) and other changing variables (known also as independent variables). Expressed differently, regression calculates numerous variables to predict an outcome or score.

A simple and practical way to understand regression is to consider the scatterplot below:

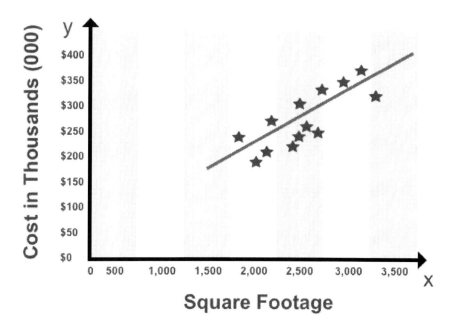

Square Footage

The two quantitative variables you see above are **house cost** and **square footage**. House value is measured on the vertical axis (x) in ($ thousands), and square footage is expressed along the horizontal axis (y). Each data point represents one paired measurement of both 'square footage' and 'house cost'.

As you can see, there are 13 data points in this graph representing 13 houses within one particular suburb. To apply regression to this example, we simply draw a straight line through the data points as seen above.

But how do we know where to draw the straight line? There any many ways we could split the data points. For linear regression, the goal is to draw a straight line that best fits all the points on the graph, with the minimum distance possible from each point to the regression line.

This means that if you were to draw a vertical line from the regression line to every data point on the graph, the distance of each point would equate to the smallest possible distance of any potential regression line.

As you can see also, the linear regression line is straight – hence it's naming. If the line were not straight, it would be known as non-linear regression, but we will get to that in a moment.

Another important feature of regression is **slope**. The slope can be simply calculated by referencing the regression line. As one variable (x or y) increases, you can expect the other variable will increase to the average value denoted by the regression line. The slope is therefore very useful in forming predictions.

The closer the data points are to the regression line, the more accurate your prediction will be. If there is a greater degree of deviation in the distance between the data points and your regression line, then the less accurate your slope will be in its final predictive ability.

Do note that this particular example applies to a bell-curve, where the data points are generally moving from left-to-right in an ascending order. The same linear regression approach does not apply to all scatterplot scenarios. In other cases you will need to use different regression techniques – beyond linear.

There are various types of regression algorithms, including multiple linear regression and non-linear regression.

Linear regression

An easy way to get started with linear regression is on Microsoft Excel or Google Sheets. Below are instructions to create a linear regression line on Google Sheets.

1. Open a spreadsheet in Google Sheets.

2. Enter your data into two rows (x and y). See image below depicting how your data rows should appear.

3. Select a scatterplot chart. In the top right corner, click the Down arrow.

4. Click **'Advanced edit'**.

5. Click **'Customization'** and scroll down to the **'Trendline'** section. If for some reason you don't see the trendline option, it means that your data doesn't have X and Y coordinates and a trendline cannot be added.

6. Click the menu next to **'Trendline.'**

7. Select **'Linear'**

8. Click Update.

Done!

Example

X	23	34	35	64	70	65	63
Y	4	6	7	8	9	13	14

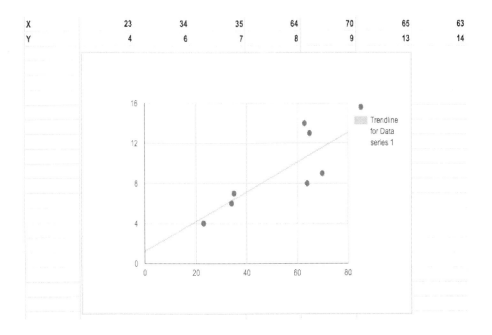

Linear regression by hand:

$$a = \frac{(\Sigma y)\,(\Sigma x^2) - (\Sigma x)(\Sigma xy)}{n(\Sigma x^2) - (\Sigma x)^2}$$

$$b = \frac{n(\Sigma xy) - (\Sigma x)(\Sigma y)}{n(\Sigma x^2) - (\Sigma x)^2}$$

This may look intimidating at first but I can assure you it's much easier after the first practice-run! Let's try a real-life scenario.

In the following table we have the cost (X) of individual keywords available for purchase on Google Adwords and total clicks per day (Y). In the second column is the cost of individual keywords (X), and in the third column is total clicks per day (Y).

	CPC (X)	CLICKS (Y)	XY	X^2	Y^2
1	2.3	89	204.7	5.25	7921
2	2.1	63	132.3	4.41	3969
3	2.5	71	177.5	6.25	5041
4	4.5	70	315	20.25	4900
5	5.9	80	472	34.81	6400
6	4.1	89	364.9	16.81	7921
7	8.9	150	1335	79.21	22500
Σ (Total)	30.3	612	3001.4	166.9	58652

The fourth column calculates the value of x multiplied by the y value

The fifth column calculates the value of x squared

The sixth column calculates the value of y squared

The final three columns you can ignore for now. These three columns have their values prefilled in for your convenience in order to complete the equation coming up.

Finally, to complete this equation you will only need the data available in the bottom row of each column, which represents the total of each column. Σ = Total.

$$a = \frac{(\Sigma y)\,(\Sigma x^2) - (\Sigma x)(\Sigma xy)}{n(\Sigma x^2) - (\Sigma x)^2}$$

$$b = \frac{n(\Sigma xy) - (\Sigma x)(\Sigma y)}{n(\Sigma x^2) - (\Sigma x)^2}$$

Now that our data and equation is in front of us, we can easily complete the equation by plugging in the values from the table. Remember that "**Σ**" equals "total value". So Σxy simply means the total value of x multiplied by y. Also, '**n**' equals the total number of data items, which in our particular example is 7.

For the following steps, all values required can be found in the bottom row of the table above.

STEP 1

To find the value of a:

- $((612 \times 166.9) - (30.3 \times 3{,}001.4)) / 7 ((166.9) - 30.3^2)$

- $(102{,}142.8 - 90{,}942.42) / (1{,}168.3 - 918.09)$

- $11{,}200.38 / 250.2$

    $= \textbf{44.76}$

STEP 2

To find the value of b:

- $(7(3001.4) - (30.3 \times 612)) / (7 (166.9) - 30.3^2)$

- $(21{,}009.8 - 18{,}543.6) / (1{,}168.3 - 918.09)$

- $2466.2 / 250.2$

    $= \textbf{9.85}$

STEP 3

Insert the 'a' and 'b' values into a linear equation.

$y = a + bx$

$y = 44.76 + 9.85x$

The linear equation above (y = 44.76 + 9.85x) shows us how to draw our regression line (as shown below).

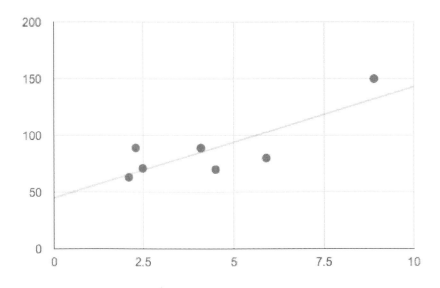

Polynomial regression

Polynomial, or non-linear regression, is similar to linear regression in that it seeks to track a particular response from a set of variables on the graph. However, rather than drawing a straight line through the data, polynomial regression lines draw a non-linear line between data points to fit the data.

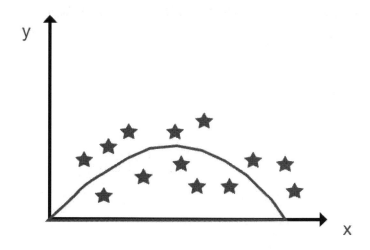

Polynomial regression models are somewhat more complicated to develop, and can be created through a series of approximations (iterations), typically based on a system of trial-and-error. The Gauss-Newton method and the Levenberg-Marquardt method are popular non-linear regression modelling techniques.

Logistic regression

Logistic regression and linear regression are similar in nature but different in regards to the problems they solve. Linear regression addresses numerical problems and forms numerical predictions (in numbers). Whereas, logistic regression is used within classification algorithms to predict discrete classes and observe which class a new data point belongs to.

Logistic regression is commonly used in binary classification to predict two discrete classes. To do this, it adds a Sigmoid function (equation is shown below) to compute the result and converts numerical results into a number of probability between 0 and 1.

$$y = \frac{1}{1 + e^{-x}}.$$

In a binary situation, a value of 0 represents no chance of occurring, and 1 represents a certain chance of occurring. The degree of probability for values located between 0 and 1 can be calculated according to how close they rest to 0 (impossible) to 1 (certain possibility). The value 0.75 for example would be considered a probable possibility, or expressed as a 75% possibility.

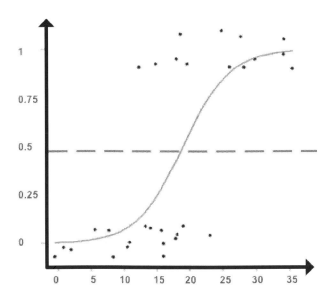

Based off the found probabilities we can assign a class. As seen in the diagram above, we can create a cut-off point at 0.5 to classify the data points into two discrete classes. Anyone above 0.5 is classified as class A, and anything below 0.5 is classified as class B.

Given its strength in binary classification, logistic regression is often used in fraud detection, disease diagnosis, loan default detection, or to identify spam email through the process of identifying specific classes, ie non-spam and spam.

Support Vector Machines

Support vector machines (SVM) is an advanced and supervised form of regression. SVM resembles other regression algorithms, including logistic regression, but with stricter conditions. To that end, SVM is better at drawing classification boundary lines. Let's see what this looks like in practice.

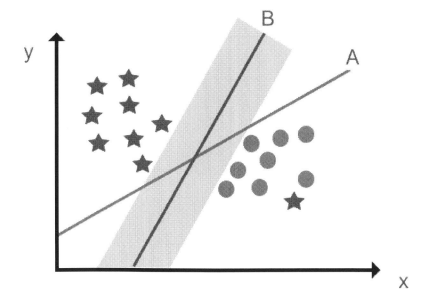

Above on the scatterplot are data points that are linearly separable. A logistic regression algorithm, will split the two groups of data points with a straight line to create two classes and that minimizes the distance between data points from each class. In the picture above you can see that Line A (logistic regression hyperplane) is positioned snugly between the data points from both classes.

As you can also see, line B (SVM hyperplane) is likewise separating the two clusters but from a position with maximum space between itself and the two clusters.

You will notice that there is a grey color area that denotes margin. Margin is the distance between the hyperplane and the nearest data point, multiplied by two. An SVM hyperplane is located directly in the middle of the margin.

The margin is a key feature of SVM and is significant because it offers additional space to cope with new data points that may infringe on a logistic regression hyperplane. To illustrate this point look at the same scatterplot, which has the inclusion of a new data point.

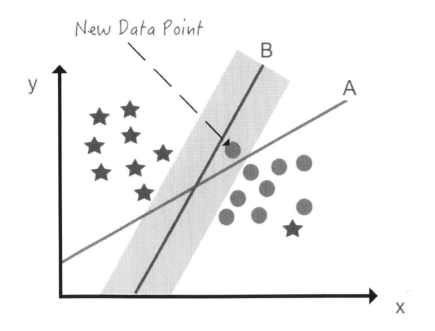

This new data point is located incorrectly on the left side of the logistic regression hyperplane (line A). The new data point however still remains correctly located to the right side of the SVM hyperplane (line B) thanks to the ample space provided by the margin.

The other limitation of logistic regression is that it goes out of its way to fit data points that are considered anomalies (as seen in the scatterplot above with the star in the bottom left corner). SVM on the other hand is less sensitive to such data points and actually minimalizes their impact on overall classification. SVM can thus be used as an effective way to fight anomalies.

The example above uses a two-dimensional example with two features. However, SVM's real strength is in high-dimensional data with multiple features.

SVM has various variations available to classify data, known as "kernels", including linear SVC (seen above), polynomial SVC, and the Kernel Trick. The Kernel Trick is an advanced solution to map data from low-dimensional to high-dimensional.

Transitioning from a two-dimensional to a third-dimensional space allows you to use a linear plane to split the data but within a 3-D space as seen below.

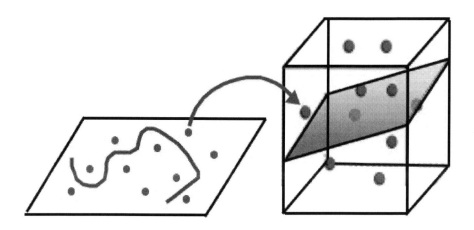

Bayes' Theorem

Bayes' theorem is a popular area of conditional probability and is widely used in machine learning. It is commonly introduced to students to solve email spam detection by determining the probability of spam based on previous results and reoccurring attributes.

Bayes' Theorem is expressed as follows:

$$P(A/B) = \frac{P(A)\ P(B/A)}{P(B)}$$

P(A|B) is the probability of A given that B happens

P(A) is the probability of A

P(B|A) is the probability of B given that A happens

P(B) is probability of B

In this equation 'A' and 'B' represent two events, and 'P' represents the probability of that event occurring. In the following example we are going to test the claims of a home pregnancy test using this equation, where:

Event A = Pregnant

Event B = Positive testing result

Let's say that the home pregnancy test is 99% accurate in recording a positive or negative result, which is the accuracy rate typically claimed by drug providers. This is expressed as P(B/A): the possibility of recording an accurate positive testing result (B) given that you are pregnant (A) is 99%.

Conversely, P(A/B) describes the possibility of being accurately diagnosed as pregnant given that you had a positive testing result. You may need to read over this a couple of times before it sinks in. It will also become clear once we complete our example.

Next, let's pretend that of the women tested in the survey sample by the drug company only 5.0% were actually pregnant. We can now discern P(A/B): the possibility of being pregnant (A) given that you had a positive testing result (B).

$$P(A/B) = \frac{P(A)\ P(B/A)}{P(B)}$$

A = 0.05%
Percentage of women that are pregnant.

P(B/A) = 99%
This we already know based on the drug company's test results, which says positive results are 99% accurate given you are pregnant.

P(B) = (0.05 x 0.99) + (0.95 x 0.01)

0.0495 + 0.0095

0.059

Percentage of those who would test positive at an accuracy rate of 99% given that 5% of women in the survey are actually pregnant, and there's a 1% change of failure for the rest of the women (95%) in the survey.

Final equation is:

0.05 x 0.99 / 0.059

= 0.0495 / 0.059

= 0.8389

Thus we can see, that although the drug company claims a 99% rate of accuracy, due to the small percentage of pregnant women in the sample data, the actual accuracy rate of successfully diagnosing women as pregnant is 83.89%.

Artificial Neural Networks - Deep Learning

We have so far looked at linear, logistic and multiple regression, as well as support vector machine, and you're probably wondering what does drawing lines through a scatterplot have to do with machine learning and artificial intelligence?

Yes, predicting values from existing data is a way to predict the future based on previous experience. But simple algorithms such as linear regression can also be completed on paper without advanced computing power.

While a number of the algorithms seen so far fall into the camp of classical statistics, they become vital to machine learning when matched with massive datasets, and combined with advanced algorithms. It is now time to introduce deep learning.

Deep learning is a machine learning technique to process data through layers of analysis and has become immensely popular since 2012. It was at this time that tech companies began to come out of the woodwork demonstrating what they could achieve through sophisticated deep layer analysis. This included image classification and speech recognition.

Deep learning though is just a sexy term for Artificial Neural

Networks (ANN), which has been around for over forty years – albeit prior to today's advanced technology. The naming of Artificial Neural Networks, also known as Neural Networks, was inspired by its resemblance to the human brain.

This analogy to the human brain often throws students. As let's be honest, how many of us are familiar with neuroscience?

Two guys who were familiar with neuroscience were the men who named this algorithm. Walter Pitts (1923-1969) and Warren McCulloch (1898 – 1969) were computational neuroscientists and neurophysiologists respectively.

These two men had a sophisticated understanding of the human brain, and observed a resemblance between the brain, which can visually process objects through layers of neurons, and this particular category of algorithm (now known as neural networks).

Similar to neurons in the human brain, neural networks are formed by interconnected neurons (or units) that interact with each other. Each connection has a numeric weight that can be altered and is based on experience.

Much like building a human pyramid or a house of cards, the neurons or layers are stacked on top of each other and start with a broad base. The bottom layer consists of raw data such as text, images or sound, which are divided into what we call neurons. Within each neuron is a collection of data. Each neuron then sends information up to the layer of neurons above. As the information ascends it becomes less abstract and more specific, and we can learn more from the data at each layer.

This is also where our shallow algorithms such as linear regression come into the frame. What makes deep learning 'deep' is the stacking of neurons that contain shallow algorithms. These neurons can contain a range of shallow algorithms, including regression and clustering. Other shallow algorithms include decision trees and bayes' theorem. Such algorithms are considered 'shallow' as they do not analyze information via multiple layers as neural networks can.

A simple neural network can be divided into input, hidden, and output layers. Data is first received by the input layer, at which broad features are detected. The hidden layer/s then analyze and process that data, and through the passing of each layer of neurons the data becomes streamlined, based on previous computations. The final result is shown as the output layer.

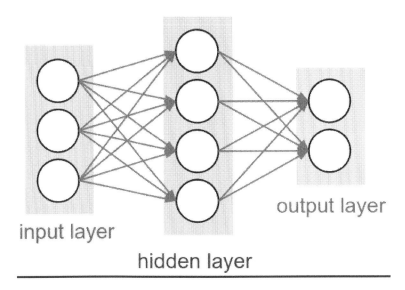

input layer

output layer

hidden layer

The middle layers are considered hidden layers, because like human sight, they invisibly break down objects into layers. For example, if you see four lines in the shape of a square you will only visually recognize those four lines as a square. You will not notice the lines as four independent objects with no relationship to each other. Our brain is conscious only to the output layer. We don't see what is going on within the hidden layers of neurons.

Visually recognizing a square is a step-by-step process. Each polyline (of which there are four) is processed by a row of neurons. Each polyline then merges into two lines, and then the two lines merge into a single shape. Via staged neuron processing, our brain can visually see the square.

ANN works much the same way in that it breaks data into layers and examines the hidden layers we wouldn't naturally recognize from the onset.

Four decades ago neural networks were only two layers deep. This was because it was computationally unfeasible to develop and analyze deeper networks. Naturally, with the development of technology, it is now possible to analyze ten or more layers, or even over 100 layers of neurons.

Association Analysis

Association analysis and recommender systems are our next two categories of algorithms.

Both categories are used to analyze existing data and identify items that are commonly associated together; such as common purchase combinations, movie combinations, or linking users on a social media network with shared attributes. Identifying these relevant or popular combinations enables companies to strategically showcase and recommend items to customers and increase their key performance metrics, including sales, traffic growth or user engagement.

While association analysis and recommender systems resemble each other in their goal to increase conversion via analyzing popular combinations, they *are* distinctly different. They are different both in regards to their input data and in their unit of aggregation (time).

The unit of aggregation or time for association analysis is the current session. A current session could be the video clip you are watching now on YouTube or this week's visit to a Walmart store.

Your previous sessions, however, are not included as input data. In association analysis, the algorithm has no idea what videos you watched previously on YouTube or what you bought at

Walmart last week. Association analysis focuses solely on the current session and is impervious to historical data about the individual user

An example of association analysis could be an e-commerce store customizing promotions on their checkout page. For instance, when a customer purchases BBQ tongs, they are subsequently offered a promotional price on a bag of charcoal. The e-commerce website does not know anything about the user's previous purchasing behavior, including whether the user has previously purchased charcoal. Nor does the e-commerce site know whether the user's BBQ is electric or charcoal-fuelled, or whether the user *even* has a BBQ.

As a generic recommendation mechanism, the sole focus of association analysis is on identifying relationships between items in the dataset. Association analysis renders itself most effectively to offline retail, as there is typically no on-record information about customers' previous sessions.

Retailers conduct association analysis on items commonly purchased together and use this information to dictate store layout and what products are showcased together. For example, research has shown that flashlights and essential supplies such as bottles of water are an effective product combination in the lead-up to a storm.

The ultimate aim is to maximize the number of products that go into a customer's basket. This is why association analysis also gets the name of market basket analysis.

Whereas association analysis knows nothing about the user's previous sessions, recommender systems absorb and aggregate the user's previous sessions directly into its calculations. This allows for a much more personalized approach to recommending items. We will cover this further in the next chapter.

To conduct association analysis the first step is to construct a **frequent itemsets** (X). Frequent itemsets are a combination of items that regularly appear together, or have an affinity for each other. The combination could be one item with another single item.

To create a frequent itemset, we must first calculate support (SUPP). This calculates how common an individual item or set of items are within the dataset.

Support can be calculated by dividing X by T, where X is how often an individual item appears in the dataset and T is your total number of transactions. For example, if bread buns only feature in 6 of a total of 10 transactions, then the support for that item will be $6/10 = 0.6$

If sausages appear in 8 of 10 transactions, the support for sausages is 0.8.

An itemset could also be multiple items, such as bread buns and onions. In this case, the support would be calculated using the same formula of X over T. In other words, how often do bread buns and onions appear together in the same transaction.

In order to save time and to enable you to focus on items with higher support, you need to set a minimum level known as **minimal support** or **minsup**. Applying minsup will allow you to ignore low-level cases of support. For example, you may ignore itemsets with support of less than 0.1.

When an itemset like bread buns and onions passes the minimum support, it gives us our frequent itemset.

The final step in association analysis is **rule generation**. Rule generation is a collection of if/then statements, in which you calculate what is known as confidence. Confidence is a metric similar to conditional probability.

This is expressed as (A => B).

A is the first item purchased or consumed. B is the subsequent item purchased or consumed given that A has also been purchased/consumed.

Following with our supermarket analogy, let's say 'A' is 'bread buns', and 'B' is 'sausages'.

Bread buns => Sausages

This means that if bread buns are purchased, what is the subsequent likelihood of sausages being purchased in the same transaction.

Alternatively, the combination could be two or more items with one or more other items. IE, Bread buns + onions => Sausages. Which means what is the likelihood of sausages being purchased given that bread buns and onions are already in the customer's basket.

The calculation of confidence is as follows: Supp(X U Y) / Supp(X)

Where U = union. In this example, let's say that bread buns and sausages appear in 4/10 transactions. Their combined support is 0.4

0.4/0.6 = 0.66

The confidence of sausages appearing in the same transaction as bread buns is thus 0.66, or 66%.

Similar to minimal support, we can also set a minimum level of confidence known as **minimal confidence**, which will enable us to ignore low-level cases of support.

If the association rule of bread buns => sausages passes minimum confidence, it is known as a strong association rule.

Numerous machine learning models can be applied to

conduct association analysis. Below is a list of the most common algorithms:

- Apriori

- Eclat (equivalence class transformations)

- FP-growth (frequent pattern)

- RElim (recursive elimination)

- SaM (split and merge)

- JIM (Jaccard itemset mining)

The most common algorithm model is Apriori. Apriori is applied to calculate support for itemsets one item at a time. It thereby finds the support of one item (how common is that item in the dataset) and determines whether there is support for that item.

If the support happens to be less than the designated minimum support amount (minsup) that you have set, the item will be ignored. Apriori will then move on to the next item and evaluate the minsup value and determine whether it should hold on to the item or ignore it and move on.

After the algorithm has completed all single-item evaluations, it will transition to processing two-item itemsets. The same minsup criteria is applied to gather items that meet the minsup value. As you can probably guess, it then proceeds to analyze three-item combinations and so on.

The downside of the Apriori method is that the computation time can be slow, demanding on computation resources, and can grow exponentially in time and resources at each round of analysis. This approach can thus be inefficient in processing large data sets.

The most popular alternative is Eclat. Eclat again calculates support for a single itemset but should the minsup value be successfully reached, it will then proceed directly to adding an additional item (now a two-item itemset).

This is different to Apriori, which would move to process the next single item, and process all single items first. Eclat, on the other hand, will seek to add as many items to the original single item as it can, until it fails to reach the set minsup.

This approach is faster and less intensive in regards to computation and memory but the itemsets produced are long and difficult to manipulate. As a data scientist, you thus need to form a decision on which algorithm to apply and factor in the trade-off in benefits.

Recommender Systems

Recommender systems differ to association analysis in that they are personalized. They focus on the aggregate behaviour and historical relationship between the user/consumer and the items available.

The two most popular and commonly used variants of recommender systems are content-based and collaborative filtering.

1. Content-based

Content-based filtering recommends items to a user based on similar items in line with their purchasing behavior.

Content-based filtering relies on both a description of the item (meta data), and profiling of user preferences. Under this model, products need to be adequately described in the form of keywords/meta data, and likewise user preferences need to be known and recorded.

User preferences can be determined by examining past purchasing/consumption behavior, browsing history, and personal details such as gender, location, nationality, and hobbies or interests. From information gleaned about the user, the algorithm can then compare that data with the description of items available and predict items to suggest to the user. As long as items are properly tagged and there is sufficient data regarding the individual user and their previous behavior, content-based filtering can be highly effective.

The downside of this approach is that while recommendations are generally highly accurate, they are limited in variety and rely heavily on specific item and user descriptions. For platforms with massive amounts of items, this can involve considerable upfront effort to properly describe new items.

2. Collaborative filtering

Collaborative filtering recommends items to a user based on predictions formed by collecting and analyzing other user's historical purchase or consumption behavior. A common way of expressing this is: People who buy x also buy y.

Indicators of user interest include product ratings, likes, traffic, purchases, conversions, time-on-page, and viewing habits (ie. watching a video or film to the end).

Collaborative filtering can be seen all across the Internet, and Amazon's own product recommender system is a popular example. Social media sites such as Facebook, Twitter and LinkedIn also utilize collaborative filtering to recommend groups and social connections to users based on similar group memberships and the social connections of other users in a given network.

Collaborative filtering recommenders are typically designed to generate results from users with shared interests. For instance, online music platform Soundify knows that fans of hard metal music who enjoy listening to Song A also enjoy listening to Song B. Soundify then determines that you also fit the user category of heavy metal enthusiast based on your previous listening habits. Soundify will thus recommend that you listen to Song B after listening to Song A based on similar user preferences.

A primary advantage of collaborative filtering is that because it analyzes user behavior, it doesn't need to rely on a complex understanding of the item itself, and the specific attributes of the item it is recommending. It is also more flexible at reacting to changes in user/consumer behavior over the long-term, though it can be negatively susceptible to short-term changes in fashion, pop culture, and lifestyle design.

A challenge and potential downside to using a collaborative filtering approach is that such systems require a large amount of upfront data. Additionally, the scalability of such systems can become computationally challenging for platforms with millions of users.

Finally, collaborative filtering is highly vulnerable to people doing the wrong thing and gaming the system. This could entail driving fake traffic to items, fabricating fake user, or generally creating a system of actions to cheat the system, also known as a shilling attack.

One approach to minimalize this issue is to limit analysis to user purchases, rather than browsing habits, as the former is more difficult to fabricate. That said, fake online purchases are still rampant in places like China and malicious groups are becoming evermore elaborate in their tactics to game recommender systems.

Mitigating the influence of shilling attacks in machine learning is consequently a highly topical, and potentially lucrative area of study to get into.

3. The hybrid approach

An alternative technique to solely relying on collaborative and content-based filtering is what is known as the hybrid approach. This third approach draws on both collaborative and content-based filtering techniques in order to effecting form recommendations to users. The flexibility of this approach helps to soften the potential downsides of content-based and collaborative filtering techniques through its combined approach.

In practice, a hybrid approach recommender can be implemented by separating content-based and collaborative filtering and combining their predictions, or by creating a unified and integrated approach. Many popular online platforms including Netflix use a hybrid approach.

Collaborative filtering can be performed both by k-nearest neigbors and the pearson correlation.

Decision Trees

Neural networks have been touted in some corners as the ultimate machine learning algorithm. This is due to the fact that neural networks can be applied to far more machine learning scenarios than any other technique, and secondly because neural networks integrate such a large range of algorithms into their neurons.

However, the machine learning community at large would typically disagree with the claim that neural networks are a silver bullet to solving all machine learning problems. Decision trees, in particular, are held up as a popular counter argument to over-reliance on neural networks.

The downside of neural networks is that they are both data intensive and demanding on computational resources. Decisions trees on the other hand bring with them a high level of efficiency, at low cost, and are uniquely visual. These three benefits make this simple algorithm highly effective at solving classification problems in machine learning.

As a supervised form of learning, decision trees work by taking a sample dataset that includes classification results, and returns a visual tree mapping the entire classification process. A decision tree will not only break down data and explain how a classification was formulated, but it also produces a neat visual flowchart you could potentially print off and show to people.

The ability to visually see the classification process is extremely unique in comparison to other machine learning algorithms. This visual element is particularly useful in industry and can be applied to a wide range of business scenarios. Real-life examples include picking a scholarship recipient, assessing an applicant for a home loan, predicting e-commerce sales, or selecting a job applicant.

Source: http://blog.akanoo.com/tag/decision-tree-example/

When a customer or applicant asks you why they weren't selected for a particular scholarship, home loan, or job etc., you can pass the decision tree to them so they can see the decision making process.

When creating a decision tree the aim at each step or branch of the tree is to minimize the level of data entropy. Entropy is a mathematical term that explains the measure of variance in the data amongst different classes. For example, if nine out of ten of your friends prefer basketball then this equates to low entropy – because there is low variance amongst your friends' preferences. If on the other hand you have three friends who prefer basketball, two who prefer football, one who prefers swimming and five who prefer baseball then your entropy is naturally going to be high.

If there is no variance at all then entropy is classed as zero. Thus, if all 10 friends prefer basketball then your entropy is zero.

Returning to decision trees, we want to pick an algorithm that can reduce the level of entropy at each layer of the tree. One such popular algorithm is the Iternative Dichotomizer (ID3) algorithm, invented by J.R. Quinlan. This was one of three decision tree implementations developed by Quinlan, hence the '3'.

ID3 applies entropy to determine which attribute to query at each particular layer or branch of the decision tree. At each layer,

ID3 will identify the attribute to minimize the entropy of the data at the next corresponding layer.

For a simple example see the data below.

Candidate	Volunteer Hours	Awards	Foreign Languages	GPA (/7.0)	Scholarship Recipient
Joy	30	2	1	7.0	Yes
Terry	20	3	0	7.0	No
Sally	30	1	0	7.0	No
Lee	2	2	0	6.0	No
Carlos	23	1	0	6.5	No
Variance	**2:1:1:1**	**2:1:2**	**1:4**	**3:1:1**	

From the table above we see that foreign language expertise amongst the candidates has the lowest level of entropy because 4/5 candidates don't speak a foreign language at all. Volunteer hours on the other hand have a high score of entropy because there are four classes within that one column of classification.

As mentioned, ID3 will pick the decision that reduces entropy the most, so that candidates become increasingly more uniform at each stage.

Therefore based on the raw data found in our table and the rule of entropy, the decision tree would be structured in the following order:

1) Volunteer hours (highest variance/entropy)

2) University awards

3) GPA

4) Foreign languages (lowest variance/entropy)

However, the sequence above is not entirely correct, because we are yet to factor in our classification rules as determined by the scholarship selection committee.

i. Can the applicant speak a foreign language?

ii. Does the applicant have a GPA of six or above?

iii. Has the applicant received more than two awards?

iv. Has the applicant contributed more than 25 hours of volunteer work?

Rather than being quantitative in nature, the assessment of students is now qualitative in the form of yes/no questions. This is therefore going to alter the variance scores that we previously calculated. For instance, as all candidates have a GPA of 6 or above, entropy is now zero, despite the variance amongst their actual GPA scores. However, for foreign languages, entropy remains the same at 4:1.

Let's now recompute the variance of classes in our table based on the criteria provided by the scholarship committee.

Candidate	Volunteer Hours	Awards	Foreign Languages	GPA (/7.0)	Scholarship Recipient
Joy	30	2	1	7.0	Yes
Terry	20	3	0	7.0	No
Sally	30	1	0	7.0	No
Lee	2	2	0	6.0	No
Carlos	23	1	0	6.5	No
Variance	**2:3**	**3:2**	**1:4**	**5:0**	

In order to minimize entropy at each layer, the four questions would be sequenced in the following order:

1. Has the applicant contributed more than 25 hours of volunteer work?

2. Has the applicant received two or more awards?

3. Can the applicant speak a foreign language?

4. Does the applicant have a GPA of six or above?

Note that questions 1 and 2 are interchangeable based on their even entropy score.

Random decision trees

However, a caveat of decisions trees is their susceptibility to what is known as over-fitting. The root cause of over-fitting in this case is the sample data.

Taking into account the classification rules of your sample data, a decision tree is very precise at training the first round of sample data. However, the same decision tree may struggle with a second round of data, as there could be classification rules that it has not seen before.

What's more, it is also possible that your first round of data wasn't sufficiently representative of your overall data, and you've already built a custom-made decision tree for the first round of data.

The good news though is that there's a way around this problem, and this is where we meet random decision trees. Random decision trees involve constructing numerous alternative decisions trees in order to select an optimal classification.

The way this works is by randomly distributing segments of your sample data and inputting it into each tree. In the wild, you will hear people call this process "bootstrap aggregating" or "bagging". The results of each tree are then voted on in order to create an optimal tree to process your dataset, or what is known as the "final class".

Algorithm Selection

By now you should be familiar with the basics of many machine learning algorithms. But what you might be wondering, is when to use which algorithm? This is indeed a major challenge for students starting out in machine learning.

The first way to answer this question is there are certain algorithms that are obvious for solving specific problems, such as anomaly detection and dimension reduction. But not all situations are this clear-cut.

Secondly deep learning/neural networks, as we have covered, is considered as close to a silver bullet as any other machine learning algorithm. This is because it can be used to solve a wide spectrum of machine learning problems. But why not then use neural networks to solve all data problems?

The reality is more nuanced. As neural networks tend to be the most data and time intensive of machine learning algorithms, simpler algorithms such as logistic regression and k-nearest neighbors can work just as well.

Thus, the computing resources you have available and/or time limitations can be a major consideration in selecting the right algorithm. In addition, the size of the training dataset will also impact your decision.

Neural networks, for example, need significant amounts of data in order to run effectively, and are more cost-effective and time-efficient when working with large amounts of data rather than small datasets.

Next, you will need to identify whether your dataset requires a supervised or unsupervised approach. If the data is labeled, then this will narrow it down to a smaller range of supervised learning algorithms. If the data is not labeled then you will need to opt for an unsupervised algorithm.

Finally, there is the option of testing multiple algorithms and evaluating their efficiency and results to the dataset at hand. This entails pushing a number of algorithms through your test data and evaluating the performance of each algorithm to find the best fit.

Shown below are the results of techniques we have studied so far, and their accuracy in diagnosing heart disease based on academic studies examining the Cleveland Heart Disease Dataset.

Sample of Techniques Used on the Cleveland Heart Disease Dataset

Author/Year	Technique	Accuracy
(Cheung 2001)	Decision Tree	81.11%

	Naïve Bayes	81.48%
(Polat , Sahan et al. 2007)	k-nearest Neighbor	87.00%
(Tu, Shin et al. 2009)	Bagging Algorithm	81.41%
(Das, Turkoglu et al. 2009)	Neural Network	89.01%
(Shouman, et al 2011)	Nine Voting Equal Frequency Discretization Gain Ratio Decision Tree	84.10%

Source: International Journal of Information and Education Technology, Vol. 2, No. 3, June 2012

The table above illustrates two patterns we already know. First, neural networks prove to be the clear leader in regards to accuracy (89.01%). Second, alternative algorithms can be applied with slightly inferior accuracy but with benefits in other areas. The k-nearest neighbor in this case produces an accuracy rate of 87%, despite its relative simplicity.

While, k-NN does demand larger memory requirement to store sample data than other algorithms, it is still a cost-effective and easy-to-implement alternative to setting up a neural network.

To learn more about algorithm selection you can check out this decision tree from Scikit-learn through answering a range of yes/no decision tree questions.

http://scikit-learn.org/stable/tutorial/machine_learning_map/

Where to From Here

Career Opportunities

Just as the Internet age created new job titles, so too will the new data-driven era we are entering.

During the early days of the dot.com revolution a similar transition took place; where many traditional administrative-based jobs, such as travel agents, or Encyclopaedia salespeople, were replaced with the creation of new job roles.

An explosion of high skilled jobs subsequently ensued in web development, search engine optimization, e-commerce, online customer service, web graphics, affiliate marketing, content marketing, and eventually social media and mobile web design. While it is possible or if not likely that a high percentage of these jobs created over the last two decades will phase out due to new breakthroughs in AI, *new jobs will be created*.

As with entering the Internet age, a similar trend is expected to follow in the AI age in that newly created jobs will demand a higher level of training and expertise. This is why we are seeing a flurry of smart young people with a strong vision of the future enrolling in online and offline courses to study data science and machine learning.

Direct career opportunities in machine learning are already growing rapidly. With the continuous innovation in data collection and storage, data science professionals are in high demand to turn unprocessed information into nuggets of insight and business value.

Due to current shortages of qualified professionals and escalating demand, the outlook for machine learning professionals is certainly bright, including salary expectations. Six figure incomes are relatively standard for data science professionals in places like the U.S, and by no means does this only represent the top bracket of industry talent.

In fact some industry pundits have rightly called out that one of the biggest things holding machine learning back right now is an inadequate supply of people with the necessary expertise and skillset.

Given the speed at which artificial intelligence is taking over almost every industry, many jobs outside of data science are also likely to become irrelevant in the near future.

The integration of artificial intelligence into autonomous vehicles, surgery and medical diagnosis is already on the cusp of replacing a massive number of jobs in freight delivery, transportation and medical industries. Even in creative industries such as graphic and web design, AI is making significant strides to replacing human designers. Grid.io, for example, is a self-standing online website created solely through AI. Popular website building software platform WIX has also rolled out an AI powered option to create and design a website based on the written content of your site.

Observers are now even having trouble distinguishing between machine/robot-generated pieces of art and music, and that produced by humans.

The BBC has a great online resource called, "Will a robot take my job?" From this webpage you can check how safe your job is in the AI era leading up to the year 2035.

The research shows that nurses for example are highly resilient to artificial intelligence as the job role entails mobility and personal interaction in a highly unpredictable work environment. Other AI resilient jobs include sales managers, hotel managers, and fitness instructors.

Conversely, other popular job roles such as bar tenders, factory workers, waiters/waitresses, chartered accountants, drivers and journalists have a relatively low chance of survival in the AI era. Already in journalism we are witnessing more of the latest financial and sports news written by machines through the timely analysis of data reports.

Linda Burch from executive recruitment agency Burch Works has even come out and said, "Within 10 years, if you're not a data geek, you can forget about being in the C-suite."

Personally, I don't entirely accept that all CEO's will need to be 'data geeks' in regards to expertise. However, I do agree that decision makers should at least have a basic knowledge and a favorable predisposition to the benefits of data science.

The rate at which artificial intelligence and machine learning is asserting itself into all aspects of organizational activities - from marketing to human resources – also means that now has never been a more important time for professionals to investigate related fields such as machine learning.

With data collection on the rise, you need to at least grasp the basic terminology and opportunities that data science presents - just as much as industry has said you need to understand basic accounting and have financial literacy to be a successful decision maker in business.

'Data literacy' is a buzzword students, professionals and leaders need to be aligned with in order to maximize opportunities in the coming years.

Working in the field

In order to work in the field of machine learning you will need both a strong passion for the field of study, and dedication to educate yourself through formal or informal channels.

There are various channels in which you can start to train yourself in machine learning. Identifying a university degree, an online degree program or an open online course are common entry points.

Along the way it is also important to seek out mentors who you can turn to for advice on both technical questions but also on career options and trajectories.

A mentor could be a professor, colleague, or even someone you don't yet know. If you are looking to meet data scientists with more industry specific experience it is recommended that you attend industry conferences or smaller offline events held locally, such as meetups. You could decide to attend either as a participant or as a volunteer. Volunteering may in fact offer you more access to experts and save yourself money on admission fees.

LinkedIn and Twitter are terrific online resources to identify professionals in the field or access leading industry voices. When reaching out to established professionals you may receive resistance or a lack of response depending on whom you are contacting.

One way to overcome this potential problem is to offer your services in lieu of mentoring. For example, if you have experience and expertise in managing a WordPress website you could offer your time to build or manage an existing website for the person you are seeking to form a relationship with.

Other services you can offer are proof reading books, papers and blogs, or interning at their particular company or institute. Sometimes its better to start your search for mentors locally as that will open more opportunities to meet in person, to find local internship and job opportunities. This also conveys more initial trust than say emailing someone across the other side of the world.

Quora is an easy-to-access resource to ask questions and seek advice from a community who are naturally very helpful. However, do keep in mind that Quora responses tend to be influenced by self-interest and if you ask for a book recommendation you will undoubtedly attract responses from people recommending their own book! However, there is still a wealth of non-biased information available on Quora, you just need to use your own judgement to discern high value information from a sales pitch.

In regards to specific careers in data science, popular job titles include Data Scientist, Business Intelligence Architect, Business Analytics Specialist and Machine Learning Specialist.

Data Scientist

National U.S Average Salary: $63,632 - $138,782

The data scientist role is one of the hottest on the planet, according to sources such as the Harvard Business Review and Business Insider. In 2014 the Harvard Business Review published an article titled, *Data Scientists: The Sexiest Job of the 21st Century*. Then in 2016, Business Insider broke the news that data science was the number one profession in the U.S as rated by Glassdoor.

The Glassdoor report itself shows that four of the top five jobs in the United States directly deal with data. These four jobs (in descending order) are data scientist, DevOps engineer, data engineer and analytics manager

So what exactly is a data scientist? Data science is a broad term, and a data scientist is an equally general job title. As a generalist, the key role of a data scientist is to collect as much relevant data as possible to conduct analysis on past performance in order to attempt to predict the future.

On a day-to-day basis, a data scientist will spend time overseeing how data is collected and optimizing the data acquisition process. From here, data scientists need to have the right strategic and business acumen to decide what questions to ask from the data and how to work the data. Being curious and having the vision to ask the right questions is an overlooked but important trait to becoming a successful data scientist.

Next, a data scientist needs to be able to step back onto the technical side to manage data infrastructure, and apply various algorithms and statistical equations through advanced programming to extract value from the data.

Finally, when results and new insights have been yielded, the data scientist must call on their communication skills and knowledge of data visualization to communicate the results with peers and decision makers.

Communication skills are vital for a data scientist because unless they can competently and persuasively present to decisions makers, their findings will fall on deaf ears and cannot be actioned. Versatility is thus key to the role. Being technically brilliant at programming and data science is one thing, but an ideal candidate will also have strong interpersonal and communication skills.

Compared to other more specialized jobs in data science, there are less entry requirements to finding employment as a data scientist. Reasonable training in computer science or statistics should be sufficient to find an entry-level work position. A postgraduate degree, such as a Master's degree in Data Science or Machine Learning, would be of enormous advantage but is not always strictly required.

Finally, data scientists are often cited as having promising potential to grow into company leadership positions given their knowledge of the company's performance metrics, as well as their broad skillset, and strong communication skills.

Business Intelligence Architect

National U.S Average Salary: $78,556 - $140,165

Bonus: $1,994 - $19,928

Profit Sharing: $0.50 - $22,510

Total Pay: $80,303 - $152,210

A Business Intelligence Architect or 'BI' is responsible for collecting, managing and processing corporate data, as well as communicating and providing actionable information to decision leaders within the company.

Business Intelligence Architect positions are generally offered to experienced data science professionals, and not as an entry-level position. A Business Intelligence Architect will most often work above a technical team or as a senior member of the team.

Their main responsibility is to plan and execute a system to maximize the full value of their company's data assets. The architectural aspect of this role – and hence the name – is to design a system that can pool together relevant data from numerous stand-alone data collection points.

Machine Learning Engineer/Scientist

National U.S Average Salary: $65,436 - $163,091

Machine Learning Engineers (or Machine Learning Scientists) are responsible for programming computers to learn on their own. Given the inherent complexities of programming a computer how to think, this job title is well paid but entails higher requirements.

To work as a Machine Learning Engineer it is important that you are not only creative, organized and have a high attention to detail, but are also well trained. Technical requirements include expertise in programming languages such as Python, C++ and R, as well as expertise with machine learning libraries and tools, including Pandas, Scikit-learn and Tensorflow.

As Machine Learning Scientists are often working on cloud-based infrastructure they need to be familiar with this technology, including Hadoop and working on GPU instances. Sound training in statistics, probability and math skills are other essential credentials.

Business Analytics Specialist

National U.S Average Salary: $65,115 - $128,800

A Business Analytics Specialist straddles both the business and technical aspects of machine learning to implement a strategy set by the company's BI architecture. If a company does not have the resources to hire a BI Architect and implement a customized architecture, then a Business Analytics Specialist will rely on third party software products to integrate business analytics capabilities into the company.

Open Online Learning

The online word is abuzz with open online learning, and machine learning stacks up as one of the most popular subject streams on this emerging new education medium.

Open online learning differs to online degrees offered by universities, such as Georgia Tech or MIT, in that they can be taken over a flexible period of time – or on-demand so to speak. In addition, they typically don't have a selective application process, and academic credit is not offered. Their advantages are low cost, flexibility, low barriers to entry, and a video-based curriculum that makes learning far more engaging.

Three popular online study platforms for machine learning are Udacity, Coursera, and Udemy. Udacity and Coursera are generally cited as the most rigorous, and the most respected in regards to certification.

The Coursera courses excel in offering a well-put together video-based curriculum on a range of machine learning topics, including introductory to advanced courses. Coursera Co-founder and Stanford Associate Professor Andrew Ng's Machine Learning (www.coursera.org/learn/machine-learning) course is an absolute must for newcomers to machine learning, and is virtually a rite of passage for anyone with an interest in this field.

Coursera courses, including the Andrew Ng course, are self-paced and can be taken online for free. However, in order to gain official certification, students must enroll in the paid version of the course, but even then it's relatively cheap. The cost is usually between USD $100-200 per course.

Udacity also offers free stand-alone courses, but then goes a step further by offering paid nano-degrees, which are more rigorous. For its nano-degree stream Udacity has partnered with major tech companies including Facebook, Google and IBM to create course materials and case studies. Udacity's nano-degrees are priced higher than most other open online courses and demand a higher level of financial and personal commitment.

At the time of writing, Udacity offers the following nano-degrees:

Machine Learning Engineer, co-created by Kaggle (6 months, $199/month). This program also offers a guaranteed or money-back employment track with tech company Paysa ($299/month). Paysa is a platform for individuals to benchmark their salary and value in the job market. A base salary working as a Machine Learning Engineer with Paysa ranges from $38,400-$231,000 a year.

Artificial Intelligence, co-created by IBM Watson, Amazon Echo and Di Di (Chinese equivalent of Uber) (6 months, $1,600 in total). This course has a selective entry policy, accepting approximately 20-30% of applicants.

Data Analyst, co-created by MongoDB and Facebook (12 months, $199/month or $299/month). Also offers a guaranteed or money-back employment track with tech company Paysa.

Deep Learning Foundation, co-created by Sirag Raval of YouTube fame (17 weeks, $599-$800 in total).

For courses charged on a monthly basis you can apply for a partial refund if you complete the course in less than the time prescribed. Udacity also offer a 7-14 day free trial, which I recommend you check out before purchasing. Also check out the eligibility requirements for certain courses, which may call for foundation to intermediate knowledge of Python and statistics.

While online courses offer flexibility, low barriers to entry and a low price tag, university degrees still remain the most respected avenue to working in machine learning from the perspective of potential employers. This is because a traditional university degree curriculum is still considered as more selective and rigorous, and demands a lengthy time and financial commitment on the part of the student. As such, open online courses are unfortunately not yet considered a direct substitute for a degree from a university.

That said, having the self-discipline to complete an online learning course is still respected by employers. Also, if you can build a strong portfolio of practical projects through open online courses, and particularly Udacity, then the online option can certainly boost your employability. Practical experience is vital in any industry, and especially in machine learning.

Degree Programs

As mentioned, degree programs remain the most respected route to becoming a machine learning expert and finding initial employment.

Machine learning is taught in a range of degrees including data science, computer science, and artificial intelligence. However, a Master's degree in Artificial Intelligence, for example, is considered very broad and is not necessarily the best route to working in the field of machine learning. This is because AI encompasses such a broad range of sub-fields, and machine learning may ultimately only constitute a quarter of the program. A Master's program in Artificial Intelligence is also more commonly used as a stepping-stone to a PhD.

For esteemed Master degree programs concentrated on machine learning I recommend you look at Stanford, Berkeley, Columbia, University of Washington and MIT. Other popular institutes include Edinburgh, Duke, Michigan, University of Pennsylvania, Toronto, UCSD, Brown, UCL, Georgia Tech, Cambridge, Oxford and Cornell.

Naturally all of the above are expensive study options. OMOSCS (Online Master of Science in Computer Science) at Georgia Tech is a special exception though, and is considerably more affordable than comparable programs offered in the United States. The program can be taken completely online as well. Tuition fees for the program are USD $7,000 a year. The lower price tag appears to be offset by the university's partnership with Udacity, and resources from Udacity are integrated into the program.

Finally, there is the option of studying a PhD in Machine Learning after completing a Masters in machine learning/artificial intelligence/data science. This is an ideal route for those who want to delve into detail on topics of machine learning that excite them.

PhD's in many countries are supported with government or university funding. However, the opportunity cost of completing a four-year PhD on a basic salary/stipend compared to working in industry with a full-time salary is sizeable.

In places like the U.S you could expect to be paid USD $30,000 a year to complete a PhD course, compared to earning USD $80,000-110,000 working for a private company. However in industry you don't have complete control over what stream and subject area of machine learning you spend your time on. Academia may therefore be more attractive than working in industry for certain people.

Further Resources

Machine Learning

A vital introduction taught by Andrew Ng available on Coursera.

The Netflix Prize and Production Machine Learning Systems: An Insider Look

A very interesting blog showing how Netflix uses machine learning to form movie recommendations. By MathWorks.

Deep Learning Simplified

A quick video series to get up to speed with deep learning, available for free on YouTube.

Learning Python, 5th Edition

A thorough introduction to Python sold on Amazon.

Want to be a Data Scientist?

A free Udemy course.

Will a robot take my job?

Check how safe your job is in the AI era leading up to the year 2035. By the BBC.

Project 3: Reinforcement Learning

Q-learning with Pac-Man. By EECS Berkeley.

Setosa.io - Principal Component Analysis

A cool interactive graphic tool that you can play around with and help you understand PCA.

Final Word

Now has never been a better time to dive into data science and machine learning.

Despite the rigorous training required, machine learning can bring immense personal rewards financially, and help to solve business and global problems.

I hope you enjoyed this book and I wish you all the best with a future career in machine learning.

Printed in Great Britain
by Amazon